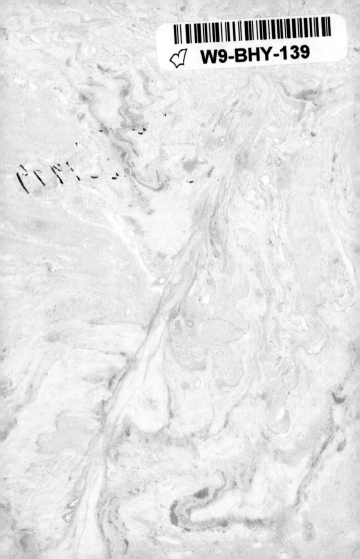

Published simultaneously in 1993 by Exley Publications in Great Britain, and Exley Giftbooks in the USA.

12 11 10 9 8 7 6 5 4 3 2

Picture and text selection by © Helen Exley 1993.
Border Illustrations © Sharon Bassin 1993.
The moral right of the author has been asserted.

ISBN 1-85015-901-7

Edited by Helen Exley.
Illustrated by Sharon Bassin.
Picture research by Image Select International.
Printed in China.

Exley Publications Ltd, 16 Chalk Hill, Watford, Herts WD1 4BN, United Kingdom.
Exley Publications LLC, 232 Madison Avenue, Suite 1206, NY 10016, USA.

Acknowledgements: The publishers gratefully acknowledge permission to reproduce copyright material, and would be interested to hear from any copyright holders not here acknowledged.
PAM BROWN, "Surprises from Devizes", "Day or Night", "Annie and Edith", "What is a Friend?" definitions; ANGELA DOUGLAS, "Sounding Board". Extract from an article in *She* magazine, June 1985. Reprinted with permission of John Farquharson Ltd; KAHLIL GIBRAN, "On Friendship". Reprinted from *The Prophet*, by Kahlil Gibran, by permission of Alfred A. Knopf Inc. Copyright 1923 by Kahlil Gibran and renewed 1951 by Administrators C.T.A. of the Kahlil Gibran Estate and Mary G. Gibran; CHARLOTTE GRAY, "Someone long parted...", "Another Spring"; IRISH TOASTS, from *Slainté, your book of Irish Toasts and Irish Whiskey*, © Copyright 1980, Irish Distillers Group PLC, reprinted with permission; HELEN KELLER, "Red-Letter Days" from *My Religion*. Reprinted courtesy of the Swedenborg Foundation, New York NY 10010, copyright 1960, USA; JOHN MACDONALD, "When you don't edit yourself" from *Bright Orange for the Shroud*. Reprinted with permission of John Farquharson Ltd. and Alfred A. Knopf Inc; WAYNE MACKEY, quote from *The Oklahoma City Times*, copyright The Oklahoma Publishing Company; HENRY ALONZO MYERS, "Bound To Us In Triumph and Disaster". Reprinted from Henry Alonzo Myers: *Are Men Equal? An Inquiry into the Meaning of American Democracy.* © Copyright, 1945 by Henry Alonzo Myers. Used by permission of the publisher, Cornell University Press.

Picture Credits: AKG: cover and pages 10, 17, 25, 36/37. Art Museum of Atenaum, Helsinki: page 47. Bridgeman Art Library: title page and pages 8, 12, 30, 41, 47. Chris Beetles: page 22/23. Christopher Wood Gallery: pages 31 and 51. Fine Art Photographic Library Ltd: pages 15, 20, 22, 26, 28, 34, 39, 42, 45, 49, 53, 57, 58/59, 61. Fine Art Society London: page 51. Guildhall Art Gallery: page 13. Museums at Stony Brook: page 41. Scala: page 34. Wolverhampton Art Gallery: page 8.

Thank heavens
for
FRIENDS

A Helen Exley Giftbook

 EXLEY
NEW YORK • WATFORD, UK

FRIENDS!

It is a good thing to be rich, and a good thing to be strong, but it is a better thing to be beloved of many friends.

EURIPIDES

Friendship is unnecessary, like philosophy, like art . . . It has no survival value; rather it is one of those things that give value to survival.

C.S. LEWIS

Who seeks a friend without a fault remains without one.

PROVERB FROM THE TURKISH

Go often to the house of thy friend; for weeds soon choke up the unused path.

EDDA [SCANDINAVIAN MYTHOLOGY]

One does not make friends; one recognizes them.

ISABEL PATERSON

I don't need a friend who changes when I change and who nods when I nod; my shadow does that much better.

PLUTARCH

God gave us our relatives: thank God we can choose our friends.

ETHEL WATTS MUMFORD

DEFINITIONS OF FRIENDSHIP

The most I can do for my friend is simply to be his friend. I have no wealth to bestow on him. If he knows that I am happy in loving him, he will want no other reward. Is not friendship divine in this?

HENRY DAVID THOREAU

A friend is the one who comes in when the whole world has gone out.

ALBAN GOODIER

Treat your friends as you do your pictures, and place them in their best light.

JENNIE JEROME CHURCHILL

Nothing more dangerous than a friend without discretion; even a prudent enemy is preferable.

JEAN DE LA FONTAINE

The making of friends, who are real friends, is the best token we have of a person's success in life.

EDWARD EVERETT HALE

Do not save your loving speeches
For your friends till they are dead;
Do not write them on their tombstones,
Speak them rather now instead.

ANNA CUMMINS

A FRIEND IS . . .

A friend is one who incessantly pays us the compliment of expecting from us all the virtues, and who can appreciate them in us.

The friend asks no return but that his friend will religiously accept and wear and not disgrace his apotheosis of him. They cherish each other's hopes. They are kind to each other's dreams.

That kindness which has so good a reputation elsewhere can least of all consist with this relation, and no such affront can be offered to a friend, as a conscious good-will, a friendliness which is not a necessity of the friend's nature.

Friendship is never established as an understood relation. It is a miracle which requires constant proofs. It is an exercise of the purest imagination and of the rarest faith.

We do not wish for friends to feed and clothe our bodies – neighbors are kind enough for that – but to do the life office to our spirit. For this, few are rich enough, however well disposed they may be . . . .

The language of friendship is not words, but meanings. It is an intelligence above language.

HENRY DAVID THOREAU

A FRIEND

A friend is a present you give yourself.

ROBERT LOUIS STEVENSON

I no doubt deserved my enemies, but I don't believe I deserved my friends.

WALT WHITMAN

If two people who love each other let a single instant wedge itself between them, it grows – it becomes a month, a year, a century; it becomes too late.

JEAN GIRAUDOUX

I do not wish to treat friendships daintily, but with roughest courage. When they are real, they are not glass threads or frost-work, but the solidest thing we know.

RALPH WALDO EMERSON

. . . when people have light in themselves, it will shine out from them. Then we get to know each other as we walk together in the darkness, without needing to pass our hands over each other's faces, or to intrude into each other's hearts.

ALBERT SCHWEITZER

from "THE PROPHET"

And a youth said, Speak to us of Friendship.
And he answered, saying:
Your friend is your needs answered.
He is your field which you sow with love and
    reap with thanksgiving.
And he is your board and your fireside.
For you come to him with your hunger, and
    you seek him for peace.

When your friend speaks his mind you fear not
    the "nay" in your own mind, nor do you
    withhold the "ay".
And when he is silent your heart ceases not to
    listen to his heart;
For without words, in friendship, all thoughts,
    all desires, all expectations are born and
    shared, with joy that is unacclaimed.
When you part from your friend, you grieve not;
For that which you love most in him may be
    clearer in his absence, as the mountain to the
    climber is clearer from the plain.
And let there be no purpose in friendship save
    the deepening of the spirit.
For love that seeks aught but the disclosure of
    its own mystery is not love but a net cast forth:
    and only the unprofitable is caught.

And let your best be for your friend.
If he must know the ebb of your tide, let him
    know its flood also.
For what is your friend that you should seek him
    with hours to kill?
Seek him always with hours to live.
For it is his to fill your need, but not your
    emptiness.
And in the sweetness of friendship let there be
    laughter, and sharing of pleasures.
For in the dew of little things the heart finds
    its morning and is refreshed.

KAHLIL GIBRAN, "THE PROPHET"

THE GIFT OF FRIENDSHIP

I know now that the world is not filled with strangers. It is full of other people – waiting only to be spoken to.

BETH DAY

. . . to find a friend one must close one eye: to keep him, two.

NORMAN DOUGLAS

First of all things, for friendship, there must be that delightful, indefinable state called feeling at ease with your companion, – the one man, the one woman out of a multitude who interests you, who meets your thoughts and tastes.

JULIA DUHRING

Anybody can sympathize with the sufferings of a friend, but it requires a very fine nature to sympathize with a friend's success.

OSCAR WILDE

But of all plagues, good Heaven, thy wrath can send,
Save me, oh, save me, from the candid friend.

GEORGE CANNING

Instead of loving your enemies, treat your friends a little better.

EDGAR WATSON HOWE

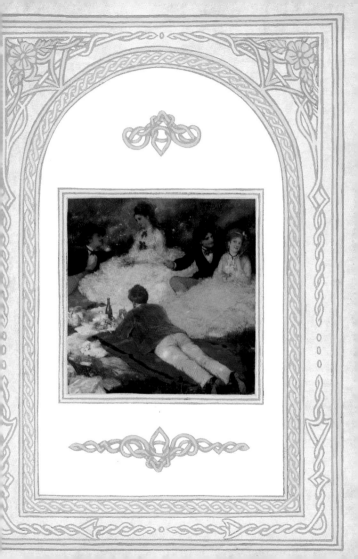

MISCELLANEOUS FILE

Just why should friends be chronological,
Fraternal friends, or pedagogical,
Alike in race or taste or color –
It only makes the meetings duller!
Unclassified by tribe or steeple,
Why shouldn't friends be merely people?

DOROTHY BROWN THOMPSON

Little friends may prove great friends.

AESOP

WITHOUT A WORD, WITHOUT A SIGN

I love you not only for what you are,
but for what I am when I am with you.

I love you not only for what you have made
of yourself, but for what you are making of me.

I love you because you have done more than
 any creed
could have done to make me good, and more
than any fate could have done to make me happy.

You have done it without a touch,
without a word, without a sign.

You have done it by being yourself. Perhaps
that is what being a friend means, after all.

ANONYMOUS

WHEN SILENCE IS BEYOND WORDS

There may be moments in friendship, as in love, when silence is beyond words. The faults of our friend may be clear to us, but it is well to seem to shut our eyes to them. Friendship is usually treated by the majority of people as a tough and everlasting thing which will survive all manner

of bad treatment. But this is an exceedingly
great and foolish error; it may die in an hour of a
single unwise word; its conditions of existence
are that it should be dealt with delicately and
tenderly, being as it is a sensible plant and not a
roadside thistle. We must not expect our friend
to be above humanity.

OUIDA

SOUNDING-BOARD

What is a friend to me? In the simplest terms, it's someone who will allow me to be the way I am and not think me totally round the bend. Someone who can tell by the look on my face when I need to talk about what's happening, or not happening, in my life. Someone who provides non-judgmental support. It is extremely therapeutic to have the opportunity to discuss problems, to consider possibilities, to use friends as a sounding-board, in order to see your problems differently. A friend is someone who needs me, trusts me, and is happy when my news is good; someone who won't go away.

I was brought up to be Miss Priss, Miss Shockable. But I was also brought up to challenge my values. My parents taught me that the world may take your money, your home, your livelihood . . . so what? Friends should be treasured. And to have good friends, you must *be* a good friend. That's what mother told me. As always, she was right.

ANGELA DOUGLAS

... AGAINST ALL THE EVILS OF LIFE

Life is to be fortified by many friendships.
To love, and to be loved, is the greatest happiness.
If I lived under the burning sun of the equator, it
would be pleasure for me to think that there were
many human beings on the other side of the world
who regarded and respected me; I could not live if
I were alone upon the earth, and cut off from the
remembrance of my fellow-creatures. It is not that
a person has occasion often to fall back upon the
kindness of friends; perhaps we may never
experience the necessity of doing so; but we are
governed by our imaginations, and they stand
there as a solid and impregnable bulwark against
all the evils of life.

SYDNEY SMITH

RED-LETTER DAYS

There are red-letter days in our lives when we
meet people who thrill us like a fine poem,
people whose handshake is brimful of unspoken
sympathy and whose sweet, rich natures impart
to our eager, impatient spirits a wonderful
restfulness . . . . Perhaps we never saw them
before and they may never cross our life's path
again; but the influence of their calm, mellow
natures is a libation poured upon our discontent,
and we feel its healing touch as the ocean feels
the mountain stream freshening its brine . . . .

HELEN KELLER

His thoughts were slow,
His words were few,
    and never formed to glisten.
But he was a joy to all his friends –
You should have heard him listen.

QUOTED BY WAYNE MACKEY
IN OKLAHOMA CITY TIMES

ANOTHER SPRING

Friendships fail some years,
blight twists the leaves and the crop is bitter.
Frost bites
or sudden fire devours:
but the root lies sound
and waits for better weather
or a storm of sleet to scour the branches.
Then we shall see another spring:
a flare of green flame
and flowers burning to fruit
along the boughs.

CHARLOTTE GRAY

WHEN YOU DON'T EDIT YOURSELF

A friend is someone to whom you can say any jackass thing that enters your mind. With acquaintances, you are forever aware of their slightly unreal image of you, and you edit yourself to fit. Many marriages are between acquaintances. You can be with a person for three hours of your life and have a friend. Another one will remain an acquaintance for thirty years.

J.D. MacDonald

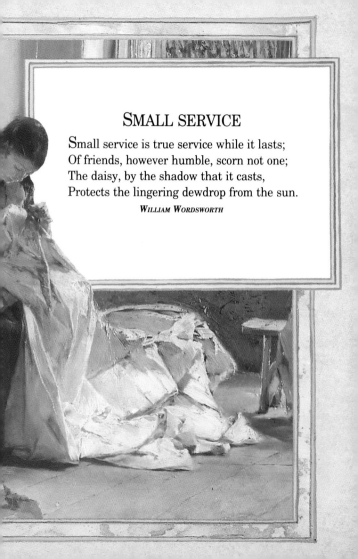

SMALL SERVICE

Small service is true service while it lasts;
Of friends, however humble, scorn not one;
The daisy, by the shadow that it casts,
Protects the lingering dewdrop from the sun.

WILLIAM WORDSWORTH

Oh, the comfort, the inexpressible comfort,
of feeling safe with a person; having neither
to weigh thoughts nor measure words, but to
pour them all out just as they are, chaff and
grain together, knowing that a faithful hand
will take and sift them, keep what is worth
keeping, and then, with the breath of kindness,
blow the rest away.

GEORGE ELIOT (MARY ANN EVANS)

The friends thou hast, and their adoption tried,
Grapple them to thy soul with hoops of steel;
But do not dull thy palm with entertainment
Of each new-hatch'd, unfledg'd comrade. Beware
Of entrance to a quarrel; but being in,
Bear't that th'opposed may beware of thee.
Give every man thine ear, but few thy voice;
Take each man's censure, but reserve thy
    judgment . . .
Neither a borrower, nor a lender be;
For loan oft loses itself and friend,
And borrowing dulls the edge of husbandry.
This above all: to thine own self be true,
And it must follow, as the night the day,
Thou canst not then be false to any man.

WILLIAM SHAKESPEARE

from "A CHILD'S VIEW OF HAPPINESS"

Happiness is if you give it away.

CHRISTOPHER HOARE, 11

Happiness is giving a little and taking a little, even if it is a mere dandelion. It is worth a bouquet of red roses wrapped in delicate lace if it is given with care.

HELEN CADDICK, 11

I like to see the persons face light up with joy, and the rustling of the wrapping paper being torn off of the present. It's so nice when they thank you for the present, and that warms you all over.

PAUL OWEN, 13

Happiness is my friend's hand.

GILLIAN QUEEN, 10

Happiness is the whole world as friends. It's light all through your life.

DANIEL DILLING, 8

Happiness is like a disease. It spreads.

SIMON ELLIOT, 11

It costs nothing to say a "hello" here and there.
To friends that you pass in the street.
It costs nothing to smile at a stranger,
Or at any new friend that you meet.
It costs nothing to show your emotions,
or your feelings when things don't go right.
It costs nothing to help the unfortunate,
Who are blind or who have no sight.
It costs nothing to be happy.
And happiness can be found.
Happiness is like butter,
So go on and spread some around.

JEANETTE ACHILLES, 15

Some people have a beautiful smile and when people see it they feel happy.

SUSANNAH MORRIS, 10

WITHOUT FRIENDS

Without friends no one would choose to live,
though he had all other goods; even rich people,
and those in possession of office and of
dominating power are thought to need friends
most of all; for what is the use of such prosperity
without the opportunity of beneficence, which is
exercised chiefly and in its most laudable form
towards friends? Or how can prosperity be
guarded and preserved without friends? The
greater it is, the more exposed it is to risk. And
in poverty and in other misfortunes people think
friends are the only refuge. It helps the young,
too, to keep from error; it aids older people by
ministering to their needs and supplementing
the activities that are failing from weakness;
those in the prime of life it stimulates to noble
actions . . . for with friends people are more able
both to think and to act.

ARISTOTLE

WHAT IS A FRIEND?

Friends don't even notice the body you are living in.

Friends are people who go on conspiratorial shopping sprees together, diving in and out of shops totally beyond their price range, and ending up eating oozing cream cakes with only just enough money to get home.

Friends don't actually lie for each other – but they put down very good smoke screens.

A friend never mentions a *thing* to old blabbermouth over the road.

Everyone half hopes there's a heaven – just to put things right with old friends.

Acquaintances call nervously to ask if they can do anything to help. Friends come and sit with your horribly infectious kids while you dash off to the Denver concert.

Friends don't have to be good looking or sexy – come to think of it, maybe that's why they are friends.

Love is blind; friendship quietly closes its eyes.

A friend is the one person who can correct your faults – and has the sense not to try.

It's easier to love mankind than keep a few friendships in good repair.

Love links two lives inextricably, like Siamese twins. Friendship lets you walk comfortably side by side.

PAM BROWN

BOUND TO US IN TRIUMPH AND DISASTER

On the level of the human spirit an equal, a companion, an understanding heart is one who can share a person's point of view. What this means we all know. Friends, companions, lovers, are those who treat us in terms of our unlimited worth to ourselves. They are closest to us who best understand what life means to us, who feel for us as we feel for ourselves, who are bound to us in triumph and disaster, who break the spell of our loneliness.

HENRY ALONZO MYERS

"HE'S ALIVE!"

Two miners in a mine in New Mexico had placed eleven charges of dynamite at the bottom of an eighty-five-foot shaft, and prepared their fuses with enough time to scramble up to the higher levels, where they would be protected from the blast. Then things went terrifyingly wrong. With the fuses burning, the first miner, Carl Myers, reached safety. But before his mate Harry Reid reached the protected area, one of the charges went off. Harry was punched down by the blast, knocked unconscious, wounded by hundreds of splinters driven into his legs. Carl called frantically. No reply. And the rest of those sticks of dynamite were seconds away from exploding, with certain death for Harry. Carl hurled himself back down the slope again, gathered his unconscious friend onto his back and started to claw his way back up the slope to safety, every sinew in his body pounding under the strain, every second ticking in his brain. As he reached the top – and collapsed to safety – the dynamite ripped the mountain. The company Carl and Harry worked for wanted to sponsor Carl for the Carnegie Award for Heroism. Carl was having none of it. "Damn the medal," he muttered. "He's alive, isn't he?"

RICHARD ALAN

THIS <u>PARTICULAR</u> PERSON MATTERS

It is a mistake to think that one makes a friend because of his or her qualities, it has nothing to do with qualities at all. It is the person that we want, not what he does or says, or does not do or say, but what he or she *is* that is eternally enough! Who shall explain the extraordinary instinct that tells us, perhaps after a single meeting, that this or that particular person in some mysterious way matters to us? I confess that, for myself, I never enter a new company without the hope that I may discover a friend, perhaps *the* friend, sitting there with an expectant smile. That hope survives a thousand disappointments. People who deal with life generously and large-heartedly go on multiplying relationships to the end.

ARTHUR CHRISTOPHER BENSON

ANNIE AND EDITH

Annie and Edith had known each other from the time when their skinny adolescent bodies were packed and laced and buttoned into their black, bustled frocks and their bony little feet crammed into button-hooked boots. Annie became cook to a lord, and Edith the wife of a Guardsman, to which positions they brought the gusto and doggedness and shrewd, pawky humour of their kind. Annie was the more volatile, having French blood, and frequently left home, with no ill effects to her family, as they knew quite well where she was. She was with Edith, getting it all out of her system and drinking quantities of strong tea.

Widowed, they got the weeping over with and tore even more ferociously into living. Edith took to Speedway, Annie to the Horses. Annie still left home at regular intervals, and the two of them went on minor rampages to the seaside, the black-eyed Annie and the china-blue-eyed Edith out for the day. Cockles, whelks, shrimp teas, milk stout and a little jay walking. Any guardian angels they may have had sweated as they wove their way among the crowds, crossing roads against the lights and giving young policemen lip. They never became the least drunk or disorderly. They simply had a very good time, frequently ending up adopted by teenagers out on the spree, being fed rock salmon and chips, and allowed to sit on the motorbikes.

They were grandmas to be relished, for they had about them a rollicking piratical air that other grans had not.

Edith died first, indignant at eighty-two to find herself suddenly old. It was a raggle-taggle funeral with all manner of unexpected people turning up, and unexpected things going wrong. Engineered, one suspected, by Edith.

Annie looked paler and more French than ever. Dressed in tight black, she wept for her ancient ally, unnerved by this abrupt silence, this assumption of dignity.

She did not last long afterwards. Ordinary people were too dull to detain her.

God knows what the pair of them are up to now.

PAM BROWN

DAY OR NIGHT

What have I got for you, my friend?

The last flowers from a winter garden, to shine against the dark. The recipe you asked for. An envelope of seeds. An empty perfume bottle for your little girl. A slice of cold bread pudding. A glossy magazine, found on a train. Scones hot from the oven. Jam hot from the stove. A small striped kitten if you want him. An armchair past its prime, to lend a little comfort to your son's first home. A glass of wine. A dab of scent. Half a box of bedding plants.

A pair of hands, a mop and comfort when the washing machine runs berserk.

A back to brace the wardrobe you intend to shift.

A shoulder very like you mom's to cry on.

The episode of a soap you missed, in total recall.

Coffee.

First aid.

An extension of your own vocabulary in times of indignation.

News of the local otter.

Availability. Day or night.

PAM BROWN

OLD FRIENDS

Old friends are the great blessing of one's latter years. Half a word conveys one's meaning. They have a memory of the same events, and have the same mode of thinking. I have young relations that may grow upon me, for my nature is affectionate, but can they grow old friends?

HORACE WALPOLE

OLD COATS, OLD FRIENDS

My coat and I live comfortably together. It has assumed all my wrinkles, does not hurt me anywhere, has moulded itself on my deformities, and is complacent to all my movements, and I only feel its presence because it keeps me warm. Old coats and old friends are the same thing.

VICTOR HUGO

IRISH TOASTS

May the frost never afflict your spuds.
May the outside leaves of your cabbage
always be free from worms.
May the crows never pick your haystack,
and may your donkey always be in foal.

Health and long life to you.
The husband of your choice to you.
A child every year to you.
Land without rent to you.
And may you be half-an-hour in heaven
before the devil knows you're dead.
* Sláinte!

May you live as long as you want
and never want as long as you live!

May you die in bed at 95 years,
shot by a jealous wife.

May you have warm words on a cold evening,
a full moon on a dark night,
and a smooth road all the way to your door.

May the road rise to meet you.
May the wind be always at your back,
the sun shine warm upon your face,
the rain fall soft upon your fields,
and until we meet again
may God hold you in the hollow of His hand.

FROM "SLAINTE!"

* *Health*